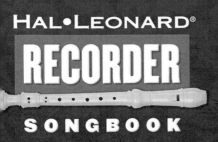

HAL•LEONARD® RECORDER SONGBOOK

BACH

18 Pieces Arranged by Leo Sevush for Recorder Solo or Duet

The particular musical qualities of these selections make them easily playable and effective for the recorder. They have been carefully selected to best suit the recorder range and timbre.

These arrangements for two recorders also allow for a variety of instrument combinations for solo or duet performance, such as recorder with piano, guitar, flute or violin. A recorder fingering chart is included in the back of the book for reference.

ISBN 978-0-7935-2764-9

HAL•LEONARD® CORPORATION

7777 W. BLEUMOUND RD. P.O. BOX 13819 MILWAUKEE, WI 53213

In Australia Contact:
Hal Leonard Australia Pty. Ltd.
4 Lentara Court
Cheltenham, Victoria, 3192 Australia
Email: ausadmin@halleonard.com.au

Visit Hal Leonard Online at
www.halleonard.com

Bourrée in E minor

Gavotte

CODA

Jesu, Joy Of Man's Desiring
(From "Cantata 147")

7

March In D
(From "Little Note Book of Anna Magdalena Bach")

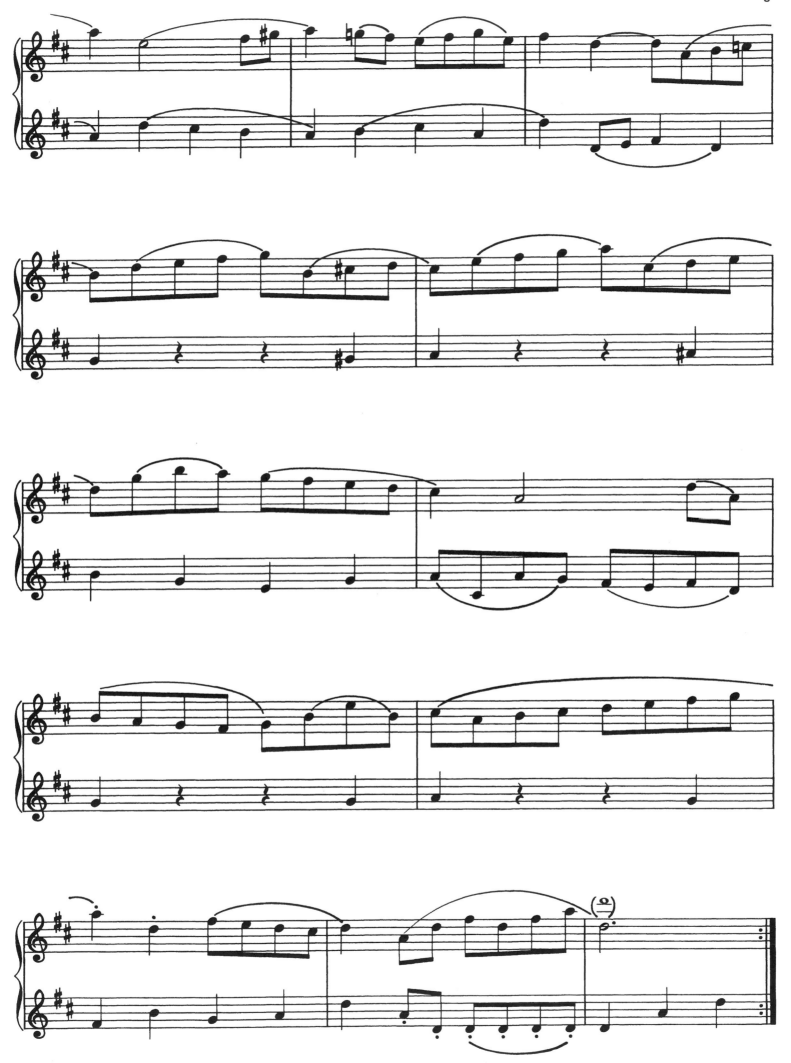

March In G

(From "Little Note Book of Anna Magdalena Bach")

Minuet In E minor

(From "Little Note Book of Anna Magdalena Bach")

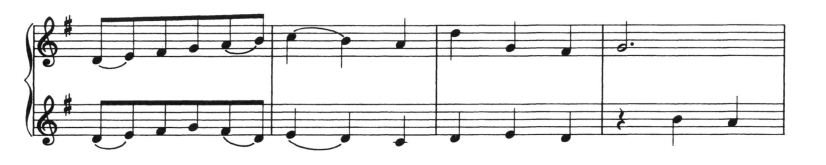

Minuet In C minor

(From "Little Note Book of Anna Magdalena Bach")

Allemande

(From "Little Note Book of Anna Magdalena Bach")

Minuet In D minor

(From "Little Note Book of Anna Magdalena Bach")

Minuet In G (1)

(From "Little Note Book of Anna Magdalena Bach")

Minuet In G (2)

(From "Little Note Book of Anna Magdalena Bach")

Minuet In G (3)
(From "Little Note Book of Anna Magdalena Bach")

Minuet In F
(From "French Suite No. 6")

Musette

(From "Little Note Book of Anna Magdalena Bach")

Polonaise
(From "Little Note Book of Anna Magdalena Bach")

Sinfonia
(From "Cantata No. 156")

Sleepers, Wake
(From "Cantata 140")

Polonaise In A Minor

(From "Little Note Book of Anna Magdalena Bach")